·HELLO·

MR JASON GRANT

Away
— AT —
HOME

Photography by
LAUREN BAMFORD

hardie grant books
MELBOURNE · LONDON

Sharing is caring.

This book is dedicated to you –
thanks for sharing my journey; here's to yours!
Finding your own style and decorating your
home should be fun, so don't forget to dream
big and use what you love.

AND A **BIG THANK YOU** TO
ALL OF YOU WHO BOUGHT MY FIRST
BOOK, MAKING THIS SECOND ONE
A POSSIBILITY.

INTRODUCTION 9

CHAPTER 1

TAKE A TRIP

Inspiration is all around you

PAGE 11

CHAPTER 2

AWAY AT HOME

Creating relaxed spaces of your own

PAGE 37

CHAPTER 3

EASY ENTERTAINING

Kitchen and dining

PAGE 77

CHAPTER 4

INDOOR OASIS

Living spaces

PAGE 99

CHAPTER 5

EVERY DAY LUXURY

Bed and bath

PAGE 135

CHAPTER 7

COLOUR ME HAPPY

Decorating palette

PAGE 197

CHAPTER 6

A PATCH OF PARADISE

Outdoor and garden

PAGE 169

CHAPTER 8

FOUND

Using what's around you

PAGE 241

DIRECTORY 279

Introduction

Most of my favourite memories are of times spent getting away – whether it was a road trip, a weekend away at a friend's beach house, a night in a fancy hotel, hanging out poolside or a big trip across the globe. Taking time out and having an adventure is a special feeling. It recharges us.

Travelling is such a great way to get inspired as it opens your mind and exposes you to new things. Of course, a vacation always has to end but that feeling doesn't have to. Why not bring that vacation vibe home with you and infuse some of that feeling into your living spaces? Even the smallest and simplest things can transform your home.

A relaxed and laid-back approach to decorating helps to create a calm environment. You don't need to over-style, and not everything needs to be perfect. Your home should be just the way you like it: a special sanctuary where you can take time out, entertain friends and family, or just sit back and enjoy your surroundings.

Think about how you live and the little things you can do to make each day special.

JG X

CHAPTER 1

TAKE A TRIP

Inspiration is all around you

I love to get away – to leave home and take a break. It clears the head. Whether you're exploring somewhere new or going to a favourite place just to relax, being elsewhere is always inspiring. Take in all that a new place has to offer. Find new things in shops, look for old signs and interesting colour combinations – absorb the detail.

THE GREAT ESCAPE

YOU DON'T HAVE TO FLY TO GET
SOMEWHERE NEW – TRY CATCHING
A TRAIN OR JUST JUMPING IN THE
CAR FOR A MINI ADVENTURE.

*It's just good
to get away.*

13

Be an ADVENTURER!

Keep your eyes peeled on every part of your journey. BE OPEN TO WHAT YOU SEE.

TOURS
TIKKI BOAT HIRE
JOY-C CHARTERS
ISLANDER CRUISES
FREE SPIRIT CRUISES
RAINFOREST TOURS

FAILFOR
NABIAC

COOLONGOLOOK

WALLINGAT

GO FOR WALKS

to take in your surroundings.

*There's something to
be said for the utilitarian nature of*

CAMPING

and getting back to basics.

I'm not a fan of a cold, minimalist home, but it's important
to consider the possessions we have. Things should be
functional, beautiful or sentimental (or all three).
Avoid clutter in your home, as it clutters your head.

FAVOURITES

weekends away

CAMPING

picnic baskets

VINTAGE ESKIES

sunrise and sunset

BOAT SHEDS

old caravans

MAPS

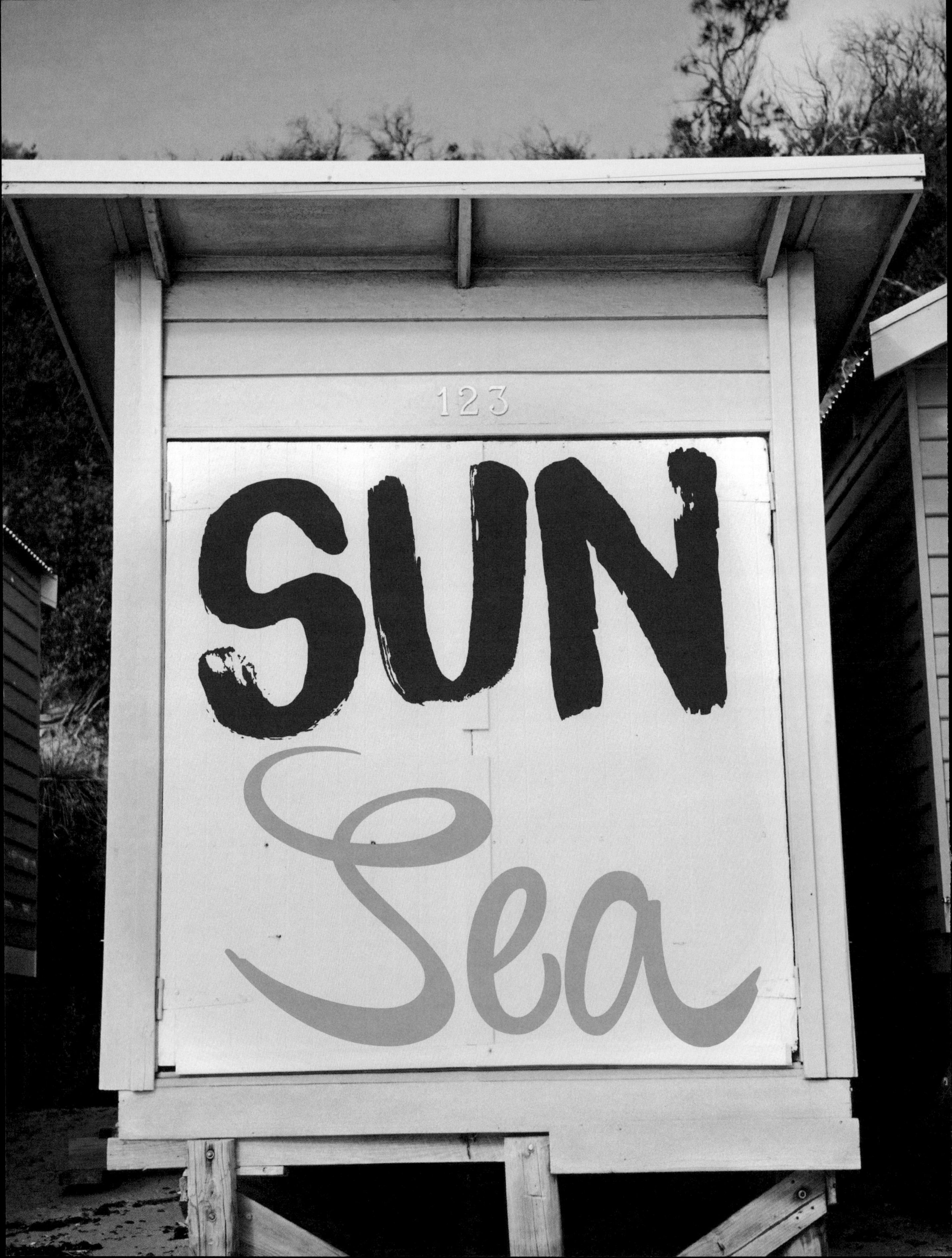
123
SUN
Sea

PLEASE—NO WET
OR SANDY FEET.

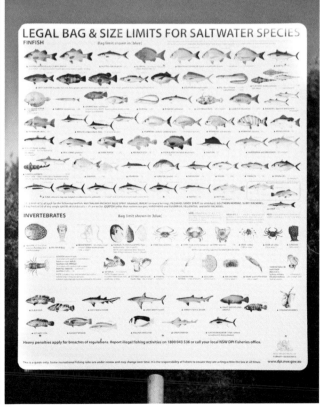

LEGAL BAG & SIZE LIMITS FOR SALTWATER SPECIES

there is

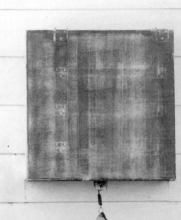

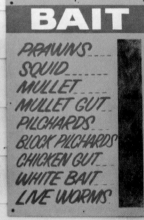

INSPIRATION
to be found ...

·EVERYWHERE·

CHAPTER 2

AWAY AT HOME

Creating relaxed spaces of your own

When we take time away we slow down, unwind and relax. It's a great feeling. Why not bring a little bit of that home with you, by creating living spaces that give you that feeling of being away from it all? In order to do this, start by really thinking about that headspace: what is it that you love about taking a vacation? What is it about your surroundings that inspires you to relax?

I love TO GET AWAY
HAVE A BREAK
IT CLEARS THE HEAD
AND MAKES FOR AN
adventure

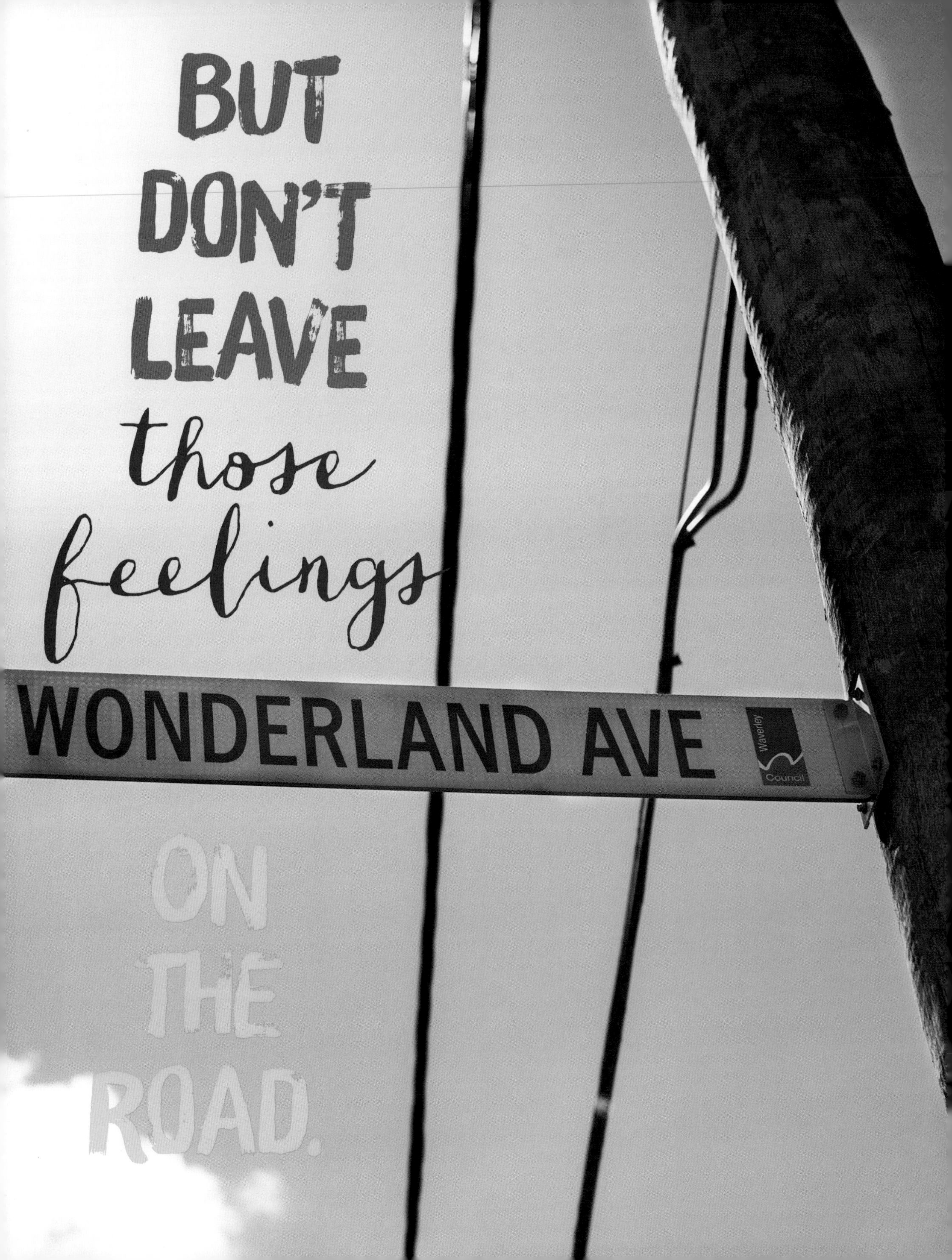
BUT DON'T LEAVE those feelings
WONDERLAND AVE
Waverley Council
ON THE ROAD.

Chill out!

BRING THAT *vacation vibe* HOME WITH YOU.

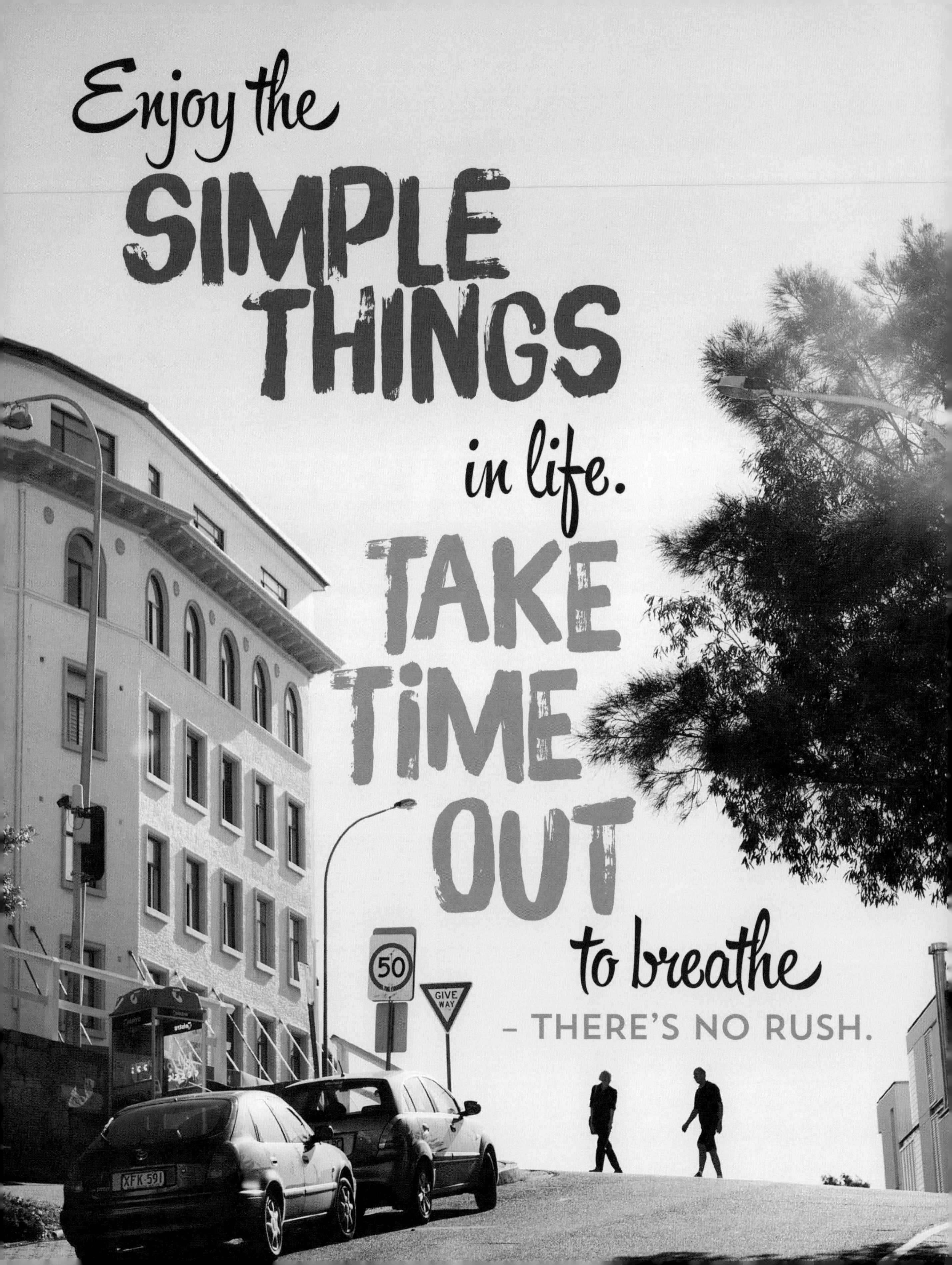
Enjoy the
SIMPLE
THINGS
in life.
TAKE
TiME
OUT
to breathe
– THERE'S NO RUSH.
50
GIVE WAY

Whenever you're away, take inspiration from what's around you. Take note of the **colours,** **shapes** and *textures* that make you feel good.

swatch

swatch

swatch

OCEAN

MISSONI

AUTUMN/WINTER
2012

Then seek out

those elements

and use them!

Reminisce

LOOK BACK TO THOSE LONG SUMMER VACATIONS.

Beachside memories

OF HAPPY TIMES

CARAVANS

RETRO STYLE

and NATURE

Bring the beach
HOME TO
YOU

The ocean fixes
EVERYTHING
IT WAKES YOU UP
and cools you down

.FAVOURITES.

FISH AND CHIPS

NAUTICAL MOTIFS

Palm trees

WEATHERBOARD HOUSES

Cocktails in the sun

SANDY FEET

Sleeping in

Pelicans

ROCK POOLS

RATTAN FURNITURE

PICNICS

The sun-drenched colours, *blue skies* and late-afternoon light of summertime fun.

Treasure your memories

Print your photos and use them to decorate your walls.

I L♨VE
ANYTHING
NAUTICAL

ANCHORS
SHELLS
BOATS
(EVEN A WHALE MOTIF)

ALL EVOKE A
JOURNEY
AT SEA
RELAXING
ON DECK

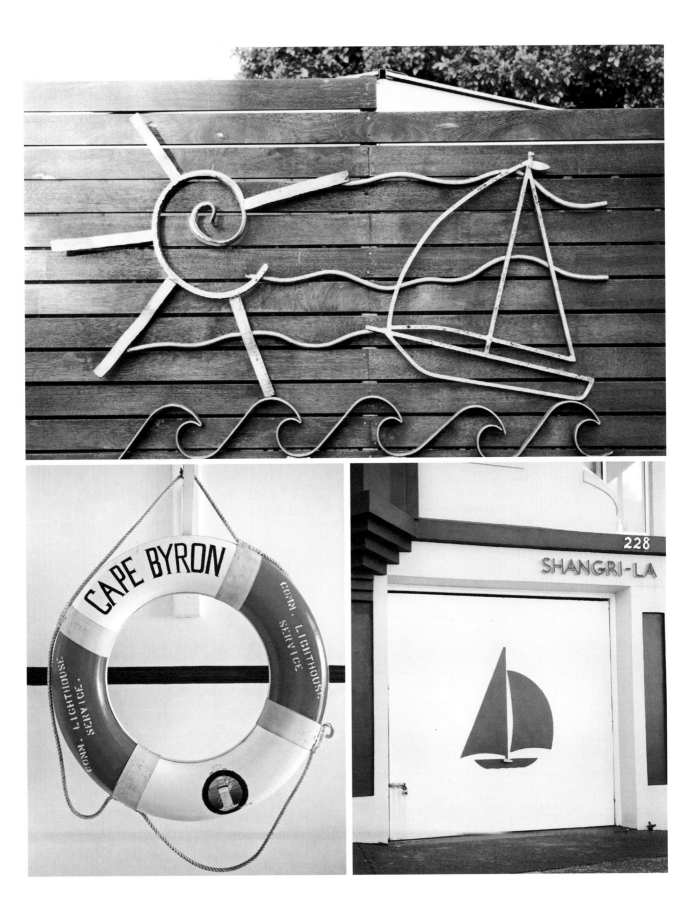

Relax
AS HARD
AS YOU WORK
and BRING
PLAYTIME BACK.

CHAPTER 3

EASY ENTERTAINING

Kitchen and dining

The kitchen and dining rooms are the heart of a home. A kitchen needs to be very functional, yet it's also a space for creativity and entertaining, food and fun times with friends. Much of the joy of travelling is discovering delicious food in interesting locations, but meals at home should be just as fun: use your favorite plates, cook exotic meals and don't forget to add some colour.

Create a FUN SPACE

for entertaining.

Embrace NATURAL MATERIALS, SOFT FABRICS,

and ORGANIC SHAPES and TEXTURES

fill your kitchen

with plants

HAVE A
PICNIC
IN YOUR
LIVING
ROOM

EVERY DAY
IS
Special

Use your 'good stuff' all the time.
Don't keep it hidden away in
your cupboards.

Rethink THE BASICS
EVEN THE MOST SIMPLE THINGS CAN STILL BE A TREAT.

Pavlova

Beat the whites of <u>4 Eggs</u> with a
<u>punch of Salt</u> for 5 to 6 minutes, gradually
adding <u>8 ozs.</u> Castor Sugar, <u>1 Teaspoon</u> <u>Vinegar</u>
<u>½ Teaspoon</u> Vanilla Essence and beat until stiff.
Sift <u>1 level</u> Dessertspoon of <u>Cornflour</u> and fold in
lightly. Wet this plate with cold water then heap mixture
on to the damp surface.

Using <u>Electric Oven</u>: Preheat to 400° then set at 250° and
bake undisturbed for 1½ hours. <u>No Longer</u>

Using <u>Gas Oven</u>: Bake for 10 minutes at 400°, then for
further 1 hour turned to low.

Top Pavlova with whipped cream and decorate with fruit
as desired. Recommended are: Fruit Salad
or Passionfruits or Sliced Strawberries
or Crushed Pineapple or Bananas.

FAVOURITES
Pavlova
SOUVENIR TEASPOONS
VINTAGE PICNIC SETS
Fancy cocktails

CHAPTER 4

INDOOR OASIS

Living spaces

Your living spaces are for relaxing and unwinding – for getting a little time away from the world. Comfort is key. Think about what you surround yourself with, focus on the details and think about what textures, materials and colours make you feel the most relaxed and luxuriant.

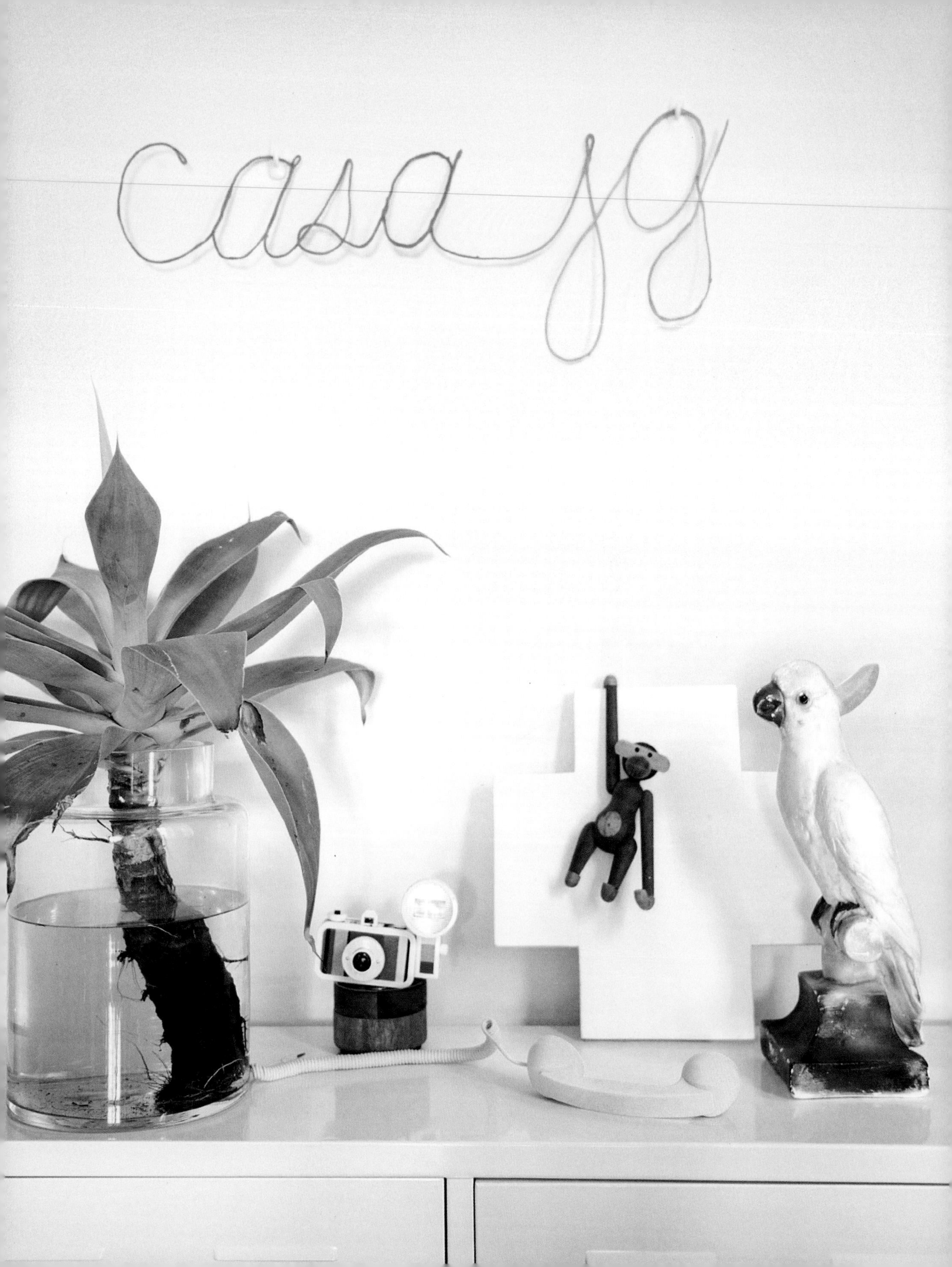
casa jg

Life is **HECTIC** so make your home **A SANCTUARY.** A special place of **YOUR VERY OWN.**

A calm living space sets the mood for a **CALM LIFE.**

(Well, at least it's a start.)

Comfort IS KEY

Embrace
different patterns,
textures and themes
in your decorating.

Not everything needs to MATCH.

YOUR HOME

is your opportunity
to make your
very own
space

It should
reflect
YOUR
PERSONALITY

CARIBBEAN

THINK
about creative ways to
ARRANGE
and **DISPLAY**
the things you love.

Create collections
OF THINGS THAT STICK OUT.
IT REALLY COMES DOWN
TO EDITING.

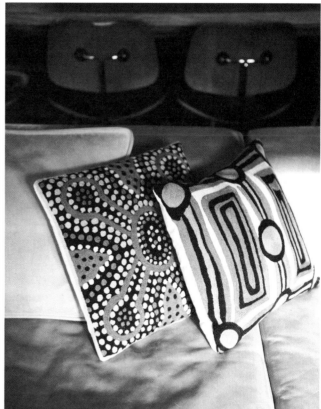

GROUP THINGS IN PAIRS, ODD NUMBERS, OR EVEN FOURS.

Rearrange your space until it feels good.

JUST *give it a go.*
PRACTICE MAKES
PERFECT, I SAY!

FAVOURITES

collecting artwork by friends

knitted blankets

STRIPES

GRAPHIC PRINT
CUSHIONS

TIMBER DETAILS

vintage sideboards

KILIM RUGS

INDOOR PLANTS

Spoil *yourself*

Flowers are an instant
pick-me-up and bring
colour and freshness to
any living space.

TIMBER FURNITURE and FINISHES WILL GROUND A SPACE and ADD AN EARTHY calm.

I AM MOST INSPIRED BY
HOMES THAT ARE
Relaxed, UNCLUTTERED
AND NOT *over-styled.*

HOMES THAT
ARE DECORATED
WITH
personality
AND
PASSION.

CHAPTER 5

EVERY DAY LUXURY

Bed and bath

Hotels are one of my favourite sources of inspiration. Whether it's five-star or something more budget, there's always an idea or two to bring home with you – it really is in the details. What are the little touches that make you feel luxurious? Whether it's soft sheets or splurging on your favourite toiletries, spoil yourself a little and bring that hotel indulgence into your own home.

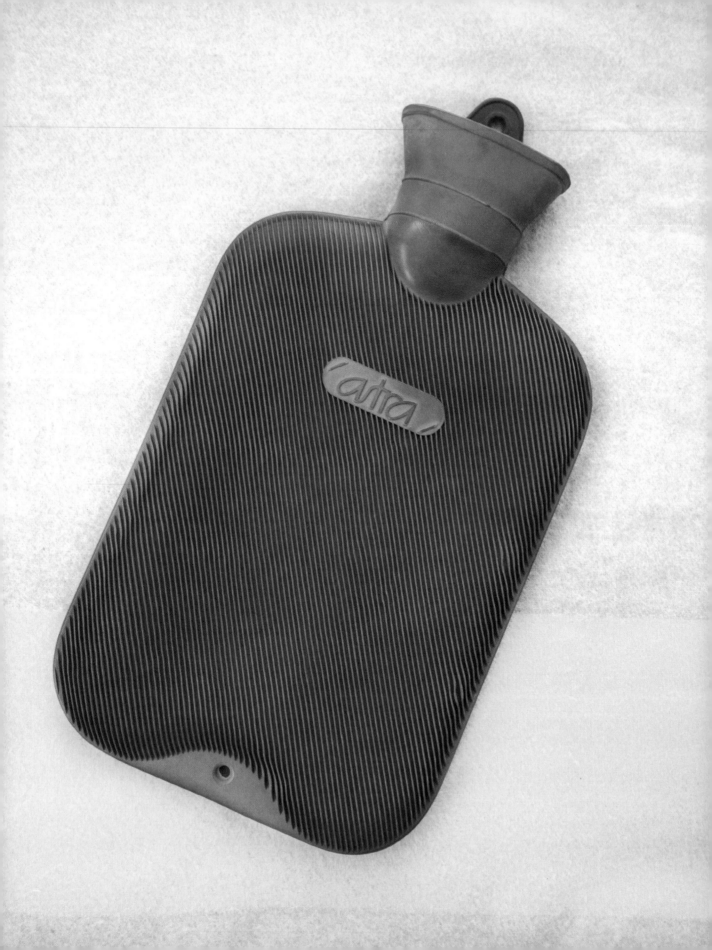

LUXURY *is all about comfort*

Bring a
little bit of
HOTEL CHIC
to your
bedroom

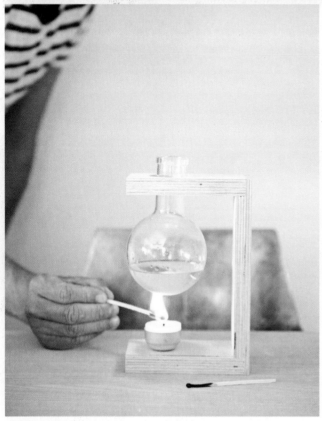

CANDLES
and
SOFT
LIGHTING
create ambience
and a
RELAXED
MOOD

Know what to **SPLURGE ON** and where to **SAVE.** It's okay to treat yourself sometimes.

YOUR
BEDROOM IS
your
sanctuary.
MAKE IT A
PLACE WHERE
YOU CAN ...

Or make
THE
WORLD
come to
you!

Inspiration

for a concept or a beautiful colour palette can come from anywhere.

Trust your eye

AND HAVE THE CONFIDENCE TO MAKE DECISIONS. TRY NOT TO OVER-THINK THINGS.

M J G

FAVOURITES

free-standing baths

coconut anything

LINEN SHEETS

BEESWAX

CANDLES

HAND-MOULDED SOAPS

WHAT MAKES YOU FEEL
Rejuvenated?

Take a vacation
in your bathroom

a place for dreaming

A FANTASY

Seaside getaway

... without leaving the house.

Pamper yourself

Put your favourite lotions and perfumes
on display in your bathroom. Look for things
in nice bottles, or buy beautiful containers
that you can reuse.

AN *outdoor shower*
BRINGS THE BEACH TO YOU

CHAPTER 6

A PATCH OF PARADISE

Outdoor and garden

If you're lucky enough to have a yard, get yourself some deckchairs and a hammock. If you have a balcony, fill it with plants and turn it into an oasis. Eat outside whenever the weather is good and use lights to create atmosphere. Even the tiniest outdoor space can be turned into a little patch of paradise.

CREATE A *Retreat*

IN YOUR OWN YARD.

HOLD ON TO
that feeling.

A place to soak up the summer sun

· FAVOURITES ·

Hanging pots

PARTY LIGHTS

DECKCHAIRS

Wattle trees

PINK FLAMINGOS

Entertain OUTDOORS

Celebrate PLAYTIME

USE PLANTS
TO CREATE A

calming

OASIS.

Get
nostalgic

CHAPTER 7

COLOUR ME HAPPY

Decorating palette

I love colour and its ability to change a mood or feeling. I am drawn to certain colours that evoke a fond or happy memory, from soft pastels to bold primary colours, all shades of grey to black and the most perfect whites, dreamy blues and vibrant yellows. What are the colours that mean the most to you? Which colours make you feel relaxed and take you away for a moment?

Decorating your home is so personal

and choosing colours to paint or decorate can be difficult. Paint sample patches on your walls and see how you feel about them after a few hours or days – live with the colour for a little while. A fresh coat of paint brings a place to life and even the smallest injection of colour can change your day.

GO NEUTRAL

Straw hats, sandy beaches, market baskets, weathered timber, palm fronds, seed pods, recycled-timber furniture.

Earthy tones MAKE FOR A relaxed home.

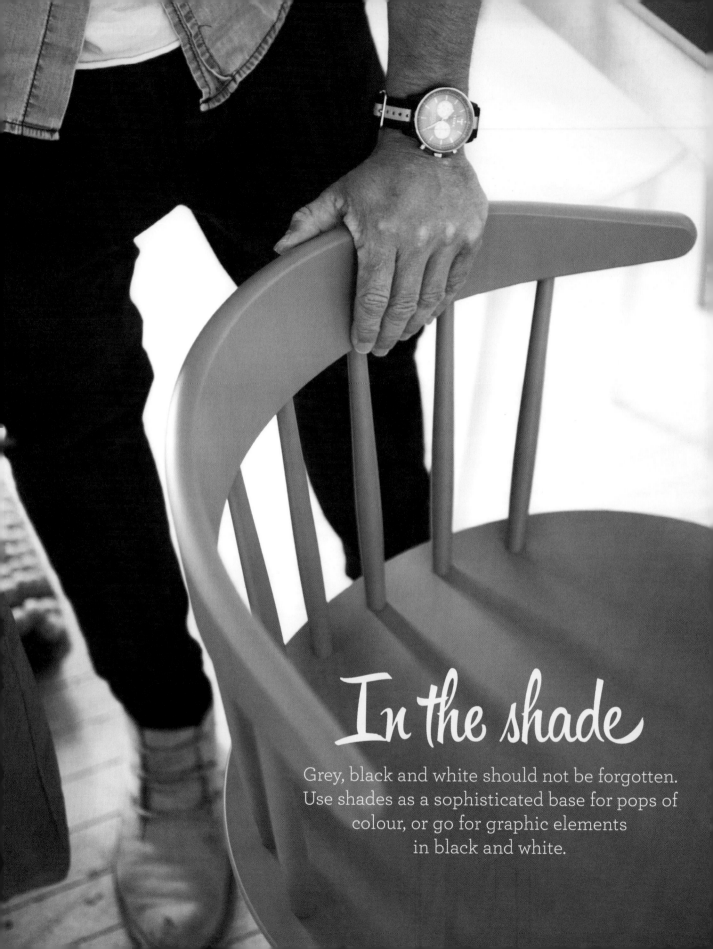

In the shade

Grey, black and white should not be forgotten.
Use shades as a sophisticated base for pops of
colour, or go for graphic elements
in black and white.

IF YOU'RE NERVOUS ABOUT USING COLOUR START SMALL

Serene, stable, strong.
Blue
is steadfast.

Natural, eco, soothing, balanced.
GREEN
is restful.

Cheery, attention-grabbing, optimistic.
YELLOW
is a big kid!

Royal,
creative, luxe.

PURPLE

is mysterious.

Love, passion,
dominance.

Red

is energetic!

Health and hunger,
happy, youthful.

ORANGE

is zesty!

I don't like to play favourites but I do love yellow! It's such a vibrant, happy shade. Don't be fooled by its intensity, it goes with most shades as an accent colour.

EVERYONE NEEDS A

POP

OF *yellow.*

GO GREEN

Purple power

COLOUR

brightens even
the greyest
of days.

TRUE
BLUE

I LOVE SEEING THE OCEAN
CHANGE COLOUR EACH DAY.

From
deep sea
blue...

...to
Summer
turqouise

NEVER
underestimate the
POWER *of*

BRIGHT
BOLD
COLOURS

But know when to employ a softer, more soothing palette.

All the colours of the rainbow.

PICK YOUR FAVOURITE SHADES AND COLOUR YOUR HOME HAPPY.

. FAVOURITES .

Monstera leaves

Painted floors

CACTUS

Rainbow lorikeets

PINK EUCALYPTUS FLOWERS

Late-afternoon light

PASTELS

CHAPTER 8

FOUND

Using what's around you

I love collecting feathers, twigs, sea glass and all kinds of things at the beach. Decorating with natural and found objects is a great way to create a vacation vibe at home, and making a simple display from found objects costs nothing. All you need is to keep your eyes peeled, look for interesting colours and shapes and think of different ways to display them. Collect small souvenirs from your adventures so that your home has a story to tell.

Go on a TREASURE HUNT.

Look for things that remind you of something; things that have a good feeling. The items you have in your home help build an atmosphere, so look for things that bring you joy.

I like the notion of USING WHAT YOU HAVE *or* MAKING DO. BE CLEVER *with the* THINGS YOU ALREADY HAVE *in your home.*

Sometimes
all it takes is some
LATERAL
THINKING ...

... *And a different*
POINT OF VIEW.

WEATHERING

CREATES TEXTURE
AND AN EARTHY CHARM.

NOT EVERYTHING
NEEDS TO BE NEW.

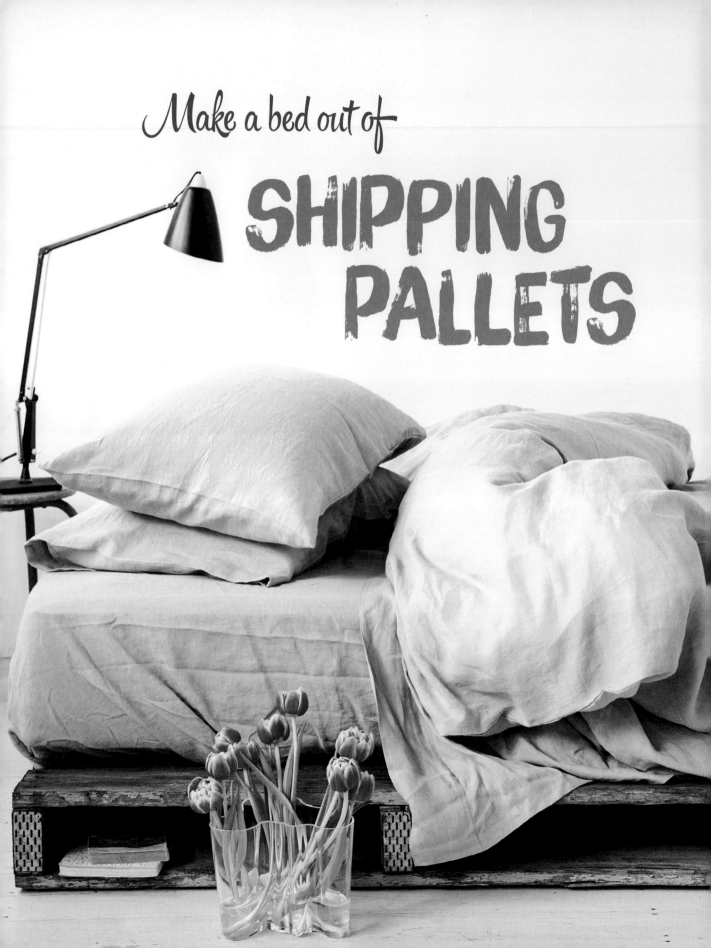

Make a bed out of

SHIPPING PALLETS

or use a CABLE SPOOL for a coffee table

Beauty
IS IN THE EYE OF
THE BEHOLDER.

Little details CAN CHANGE THE WAY YOU FEEL.

Keep an EYE OUT for DETAIL. Look for INTERESTING SHAPES, COLOURS and TEXTURES.

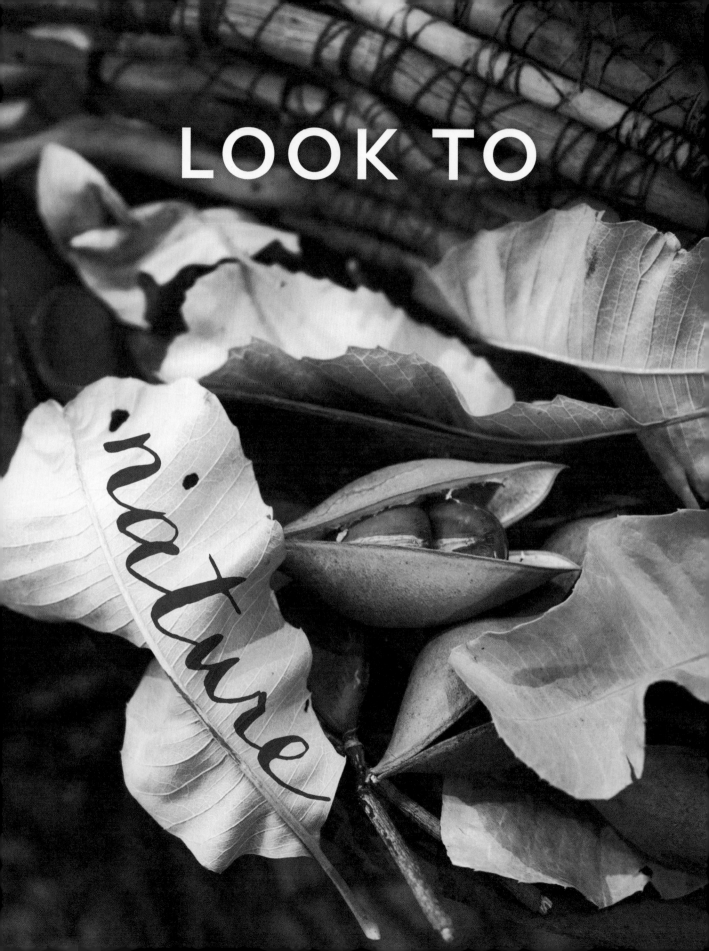

LOOK TO

nature

USE *leaves* AND *twigs* INSTEAD OF FLOWERS FOR LASTING DISPLAYS.

PLANTS WILL GROW IN ALMOST ANY CONTAINER (or none at all). BE CREATIVE!

Collect **SUCCULENT CUTTINGS** and surround

yourself with GREEN.

YOUR GARDEN

doesn't need to be neatly
manicured to be beautiful.
Fill it with strange objects to
be discovered.

There's always a
SOUVENIR
to keep and a story to tell.
Keep them on display.

Decorating

doesn't need to be expensive. Think differently and come up with ideas that don't cost very much.

. FAVOURITES .

furniture on castors

SHELLS

sea glass

feathers

TREE HOUSES

SHIPPING PALLETS

amethyst crystals

ALWAYS REMEMBER TO

take time out

EVERY DAY, EVEN IF IT'S
JUST FOR A MOMENT.

Make your home

THE PLACE YOU

daydream

ABOUT.

DIRECTORY

The following is a list of my favourite sources of inspiration. Whether I'm shopping or day-dreaming, near or far, these are the people who inspire me – I have their websites bookmarked, their addresses imprinted in my brain and their numbers saved in my phone. They all do great stuff. Make this your go-to list too!

Special MENTIONS

The following are stores, designers and artists who have all contributed in some wonderful way to what you see in the pages of this book.

The Academy Brand
academybrand.com

ABC Carpet & Home
abchome.com

Aesop
aesop.com

Armadillo&Co.
armadillo-co.com

Aura by Tracie Ellis
aurahome.com.au

Basil Bangs
basilbangs.com

Bassike
bassike.com

Beci Orpin
beciorpin.com

Blacklist.
blackliststore.com.au

Blu Dot
bludot.com.au

Bondi Wash
bondiwash.com.au

Bonnie and Neil
bonnieandneil.com.au

Castle
castleandthings.com.au

Cloth Fabric
clothfabric.com

Country Road
countryroad.com.au

Crate and Barrel
crateandbarrel.com

Cult.
cultdesigned.com.au

de de ce
dedeceplus.com

Designer Rugs
designerrugs.com.au

The Dharma Door
thedharmadoor.com.au

Dinosaur Designs
dinosaurdesigns.com.au

Douglas and Hope
douglasandhope.bigcartel.com

The Family Love Tree
thefamilylovetree.com.au

Fishs Eddy
fishseddy.com

Flamingos Forever
pinkflamingos.com.au

The Flower Drum by Holly Hipwell
theflowerdrum.blogspot.com.au

Flowers Vasette
flowersvasette.com.au

Flux
flux.com.au

Freedom
freedom.com.au

Georg Jensen
georgjensen.com

Giant Swan
giantswan.com.au

Girl & Graaf
girlandgraaf.com.au

Great Dane Furniture
greatdanefurniture.com

Guy Mathews
guymathewsindustrial.com.au

Kawaiian Lion
kawaiianlion.bigcartel.com

Kelly Wearstler
kellywearstler.com

Have You Met Miss Jones
haveyoumetmissjones.com.au

Heath's Old Wares
heathsoldwares.com.au

I Like Birds
ilikebirds.com.au

Izola
izola.com

Jonathan Adler
jonathanadler.com

Koselka
koselka.com.au

kikki.K
kikki-k.com

little nicki
etsy.com/au/shop/littlenicki

Major Minor Sydney
majorminorsydney.com

Manon bis
manonbis.com.au

marimekko
marimekko.com

Mark Tuckey
marktuckey.com.au

Mud Australia
mudaustralia.com

Murobond Paints
murobond.com.au

Our Corner Store
ourcornerstore.com.au

Pony Rider
ponyrider.com.au

Robert Gordon
robertgordonaustralia.com

Safari Living
safariliving.com

SailCorp Yacht Charters
sailcorp.com.au

Saison
saison.com.au

Scout House
scouthouse.com.au

Seasonal Concepts
seasonalconcepts.com.au

smallspaces
small-spaces.com.au

Thonet
thonet.com.au

TRIWA
triwa.com

Vanishing Elephant
vanishingelephant.com

Violet+Rose
violetandrose.com

west elm
westelm.com

Whiting Architects
whitingarchitects.com

yellow bungalow
yellowbungalow.com.au

INSPIRATION

Inspiration can come from many places. Here are some clever people and great places I go to regularly for inspiration and ideas.

Airstream Dreams
airstreamdreams.com.au

Aquabumps
aquabumps.com

Citizens of the World
hellocitizens.com

The Establishment Studios
theestablishmentstudios.
com.au

Greg Hatton
greghatton.com

Hearth
hearthstudio.com.au

Katie Marx Flowers
katiemarxflowers.tumblr.com

Lauren Bamford
laurenbamford.com

Leila Jeffreys
leilajeffreys.com

Little Dandelion
littledandelion.com

Lomography Australia
lomography.com.au

origrami
origrami.com

the transcontinental affair
thetranscontinentalaffair.
blogspot.com.au

PLACES *to* STAY

Some of my favourite hotels and sources for accommodation that are endlessly inspiring to me.

Ace Hotel
acehotel.com

Art Series Hotel Group
artserieshotels.com.au

Atlantic Byron Bay
atlanticbyronbay.com.au

The Beverly Hills Hotel
beverlyhillshotel.com

Expedia
expedia.com.au

Jonah's Restaurant and Boutique Hotel
jonahs.com.au

Mr & Mrs Smith
mrandmrssmith.com

Mr. C Beverly Hills
mrchotels.com

Paperbark Camp
paperbarkcamp.com.au

Park Hyatt Sydney
sydney.park.hyatt.com

The White House Daylesford
thewhitehousedaylesford.
com.au

THE FUTURE
IS EXCITING

Thanks

A special thanks to Lauren Bamford (and her husband Keith). You really took this project on as your own 'dream project' and I appreciate all of your hard work, enthusiasm and suggestions – you really made this happen.

My amazing team at Hardie Grant and Rizzoli: especially Paul, Hannah (my awesome book editor), Caitlin and Mark, and also my very talented book designer Kirby – it's a dream team! I'm so lucky to work with you all.

To those who invited me into their homes: Kimberly, Mark and Louella, Hilary, Guy, Belinda, Nicole and Chris, Eugene and Deb, Russell and Sasha, Stephen and Carol, Cathy, Nathan and Jaynie, Beci and Raph, Denis and Carolyn, Lyn, Greg and Katie, Mr and Mrs Bamford, Mike and Krista, Adam, and Don at the Beverly Hills apartments. From the Northern Beaches, the Mornington Peninsula, Bondi to Byron Bay to Newcastle, Daylesford, Melbourne and more: I love your style.

To the best four-legged friends: Stanley, Olive, Kevin and Bunny. And to Molly and Jimmy the super-cool VW Beetle.

Friends and family are everything; thanks to all for your encouragement, support and patience.

And a very special mention goes to Andrew, Mark and Barry, Natalie, Orlando and Brendan.

About the Author

Mr Jason Grant is a Sydney-based interior stylist and author who has worked with many Australian and international magazines, and collaborated with exciting major brands; including a signature collection with Murobond Paints. This is his second book, a follow up to *A Place Called Home*.

Follow Jason on Instagram **@mr_jason_grant** or on his blog **mrjasongrant.com.**

ABOUT THE PHOTOGRAPHER

Lauren Bamford is a professional photographer, based in Melbourne, Australia, who specialises in food, lifestyle, interiors and documentary photography. Lauren has been commissioned by international publications, record companies and advertising agencies.

Maintaining an unobtrusive approach to her subjects, Lauren has also developed a large body of personal photography work, which has been exhibited at various art galleries including the National Gallery of Victoria.

Check out more of her work at **laurenbamford.com.**

Published in 2014 by Hardie Grant Books

Hardie Grant Books (Australia)
Ground Floor, Building 1
658 Church Street
Richmond, Victoria 3121
www.hardiegrant.com.au

Hardie Grant Books (UK)
Dudley House, North Suite
34–35 Southampton Street
London WC2E 7HF
www.hardiegrant.co.uk

A Cataloguing-in-Publication entry is available from
the catalogue of the National Library of Australia at
www.nla.gov.au

Holiday at Home / Away at Home (US only)
ISBN 9781742707006

Publishing Director: Paul McNally
Project Editor: Hannah Koelmeyer
Design Manager: Mark Campbell
Designer: Kirby Armstrong
Photographer: Lauren Bamford
Production Manager: Todd Rechner

Colour reproduction by Splitting Image Colour Studio
Printed in China by 1010 Printing International Limited